London Borough of Havering

KIDS IN THE KITCHEN

Cooking Gluten Free

Janet Wheelock Balsbaugh

authorHOUSE®

AuthorHouse™
1663 Liberty Drive
Bloomington, IN 47403
www.authorhouse.com
Phone: 1-800-839-8640

© 2013 Janet Wheelock Balsbaugh. All rights reserved.

No part of this book may be reproduced, stored in a retrieval system, or transmitted by any means without the written permission of the author.

Published by AuthorHouse 1/25/2013

ISBN: 978-1-4772-9594-6 (sc)
ISBN: 978-1-4772-9595-3 (e)

Library of Congress Control Number: 2012922719

Any people depicted in stock imagery provided by Thinkstock are models, and such images are being used for illustrative purposes only.
Certain stock imagery © Thinkstock.

This book is printed on acid-free paper.

Because of the dynamic nature of the Internet, any web addresses or links contained in this book may have changed since publication and may no longer be valid.

The views expressed in this work are solely those of the author and do not necessarily reflect the views of the publisher, and the publisher hereby disclaims any responsibility for them.

This book is dedicated to my three adorable grandsons, Simon, Tristan, and Patrick, who are the love of my life.

Table of Contents

Introduction ix
Foreword xi
Disclaimer xiii
Acknowledgments xv
Gluten-Free Flours and Starches xvii

Appetizers 1
    Black Bean Salsa 3
    Baked Corn Tortilla Chips 4
    Ants on a Log 5
    Crostini 6
    Fruit Kabobs 7
    Turkey Nachos 8
    Deviled Eggs 9
    Potato Boats 10
    Raw Vegetable Dip 12
    Chip Dip 13

Beverages 15
    Hot Chocolate 17
    Chocolate Banana Shakes 18
    Strawberry Shakes 19
    Strawberry Banana Shakes 20
    Lemonade 21

Main Dishes 23
    Grilled Cheese 25
    Chili 26
    Chili Mac 27
    Vegetable Soup 28
    My Mom Makes Chicken Noodle Soup 29
    Pizza 30
    Baked French Fries 31
    Chicken Loaf 32
    Cream Sauce 33

Fish Sticks	34
Chicken Nuggets	35
Pork Chops	36
Spaghetti with Marinara Sauce	37
Meatballs	38
Macaroni and Cheese	39
Cheese Sauce	40
Sloppy Joes	41
Salmon Patties	42
Tacos	43
Taco Seasoning	44
Beanie Weenies	45
Quesadillas	46
Baked Chicken Patties	47

BREAKFAST 49

French Toast	51
Pancakes	52
Sausage Gravy	54
Scrambled Eggs	55
Hole in One	56
Banana Muffins	57

DESSERTS 59

Chocolate Chip Cookies	61
Chocolate Pudding	62
Rice Chex Cereal Bars	63
Rice Krispie Treats	64
Chocolate Brownies	65
Gluten-Free Flour Mix	66

Where to Find Gluten-Free and Dairy-Free Supplies	67
Measurements	71
Oven Chart	72
About the Author	73

Introduction

Living gluten-free and/or dairy-free is a real challenge. I needed to find ways of trying to improve my life, and have read so much information on the benefits of being gluten- and dairy-free; I thought I would give it a try. Living a gluten-free and dairy-free lifestyle has helped me. Now when walking into a store, the first thing I do is shop, not look for a bathroom.

I started to experiment with different flours, soy and rice milks, and dairy products. I wanted my regular food back, and the only way that was going to happen was to do my best in making foods that remind me of the ones I love, such as home-style comfort foods. My nutritionist told me that changing my diet to gluten- and dairy-free would help me.

So that is how this cookbook began: a quest for good food, while staying healthy at the same time. Let me remind you, though, on a gluten-free diet, you may have unusual textures in some of your foods, but should still have the flavor of the food you are used to.

With this in mind, and the comments I have received from parents of children I have spoken with, I thought this cookbook would be fun to put together as a gluten-free alternative for parents and children to work together in the kitchen.

The recipes contained in this cookbook are all gluten-free, with some having dairy-free options also.

I know you and your children will have as much fun in the kitchen preparing these simple dishes as I have.

Welcome to my kitchen, and please enjoy these recipes.

Foreword

Crohn's disease is an inflammatory bowel disease (IBD). It can cause inflammation in your intestines along with diarrhea. The diarrhea can lead to malnutrition, which can make it difficult for the intestine to absorb enough nutrients, which can cause anemia. As far as I know, there is no known cure for Crohn's disease.

Sclerosing cholangitis is a disease of the bile ducts. It is a disease that leads to liver damage and eventually liver failure.

Living with two autoimmune diseases has provided a great challenge in my life. Following a gluten-free and dairy-free options, along with proper rest, help me live a more fulfilling life.

Disclaimer

I have tested the recipes in this book and, to the best of my knowledge, they are safe for ordinary use and users.

As far as I know, all of the recipes within this book are gluten-free.

All recipes are used at the risk of the consumer.

I cannot be responsible for any damage that may occur as a result of any recipe use.

For those of you with allergies or health issues, please contact your medical advisor or your physician prior to the use of any recipe.

This cookbook is intended as a reference volume only, not a medical manual.

This book does not replace medical advice.

The author and publisher disclaim any liability arising directly or indirectly from the use of this book.

Acknowledgments

I would like to take a moment to thank those that helped make this book possible.

First of all, I want to thank my mom. The skills she taught me in cooking from the time I was little have helped me to become what I am today. Love you, Mom!

I want to thank my biggest taste-tester, my husband Jim. He has always given me an honest opinion of what my newest projects taste like.

My sister Judy, brother-in-law Terry, and nephew Connor have tested so many of my recipes and give helpful suggestions.

Thank you to Terry C. Penkal of TCP Enterprises for the illustrations provided in this cookbook. http://www.tcpenart.com

Gluten-Free Flours and Starches

Arrowroot Starch
Used as a thickener. Those that are allergic to corn can use arrowroot starch in place of cornstarch. Like cornstarch, this must be mixed with a cold liquid before adding to hot liquids.

Bean Flours
There are different kinds of bean flour available, such as garbanzo bean flour (chickpea), fava flour (fava beans), and Romano whole bean flour (cranberry). Bean flour contains more protein than other gluten-free flours. Bean flours can be used in baking and also make good thickeners.

Cornstarch
This is a starch made from corn. This can be used as a thickener. Like arrowroot starch, mix this with a cold liquid before adding to hot liquids. If you are allergic to corn, use the arrowroot starch in place of cornstarch.

Cornmeal
This is a meal ground from corn. This can be either yellow or white in color. This can be combined with other flours, or used by itself.

Potato Flour
This is different from potato starch. Do not confuse this. This is heavy flour made from cooked potatoes. This combines well with other rice flours.

Potato Starch
Remember this is different from potato flour. This is made from raw potatoes. This has a higher heat point than cornstarch, so it is better to use with certain foods that require a higher temperature.

Brown Rice Flour
This is made from unpolished brown rice. This flour provides more fiber than white rice flour. This contains bran, and since there are oils in the bran, this must be refrigerated.

Sweet Rice Flour

This is known as sticky rice. Contains more starch than brown or white rice flours. This is an excellent thickener. Do not confuse this with plain white rice flour.

White Rice Flour

This flour is made from grinding polished white rice. This flour is very bland. This can be used as a thickener for puddings and sauces, or combined with other flours such as potato, buckwheat, or corn flour, and can be used in some baked goods such as cakes and cookies.

Sorghum Flour

This flour is high in soluble fiber. This works well with rice flours and gives them flavor and body. Sorghum is of the same family as sugar cane, rice, and corn.

Soy Flour

This flour is from ground soybeans. This flour is high in fat and protein and works best when combined with other flours, such as rice flour.

Tapioca Flour

This is also known as tapioca starch. I went into the local Healthy Alternatives store one day and tried to find both of these items, only to find they were the same thing. This flour is made from the cassava root. It works best in combination with other flours, such as white rice flour or potato flour.

Xanthan Gum

This is used as a substitute for wheat gluten in gluten-free breads, pastas, and other flour-based food products. Those who suffer from gluten allergies should look for xanthan gum as an ingredient on the label.

Appetizers

Black Bean Salsa

1 15-oz. can black beans
1/2 medium red onion diced
3 tsp garlic minced
3 tsp cilantro chopped
2 medium tomatoes diced
Salt and pepper to taste

Rinse beans under cold water and drain. Mix beans with the rest of the ingredients and let flavors marry together in the refrigerator 1 hour. Serve chilled or at room temperature with gluten-free tortilla chips.

Optional: Add extra diced red onion and cilantro for a spicier version.

Baked Corn Tortilla Chips

Corn tortillas (soft)
Gluten-free cooking spray
Salt

Preheat oven to 350 degrees. Line a baking sheet with aluminum foil, shiny side down. Spray the tortillas with gluten-free cooking spray on both sides. Cut each into 8 triangles (I use a pizza cutter for mine). Sprinkle a very small amount of salt on tortillas (just a pinch). Lay flat on cookie sheet, leaving a little space between each one. Bake for 12-15 minutes or until desired doneness is achieved. Remember, ovens vary. Start checking these at around 9 minutes.

Optional: You can put whatever spices you like on these. Try a sprinkling of Italian seasoning or a little bit of salt and pepper.

Ants on a Log

6 celery stalks
Cream cheese
Raisins

Clean celery and cut each stalk into 3 pieces. Fill with cream cheese and sprinkle with raisins.

Makes 18.

Optional: Try peanut butter in place of cream cheese.

For those going dairy-free, use Tofutti cream cheese.

Crostini

1 loaf Schar gluten-free baguette
Extra virgin olive oil
Salt and pepper
One to two garlic cloves cut in half

Preheat oven to 375 degrees. Slice baguette into 1" pieces. Brush olive oil on both sides of each piece. Place on a cookie sheet. Sprinkle with salt and pepper. Toast for 10 to 12 minutes, turning halfway through. As soon as you take these out of the oven, rub with a clove of garlic on one each side. Serve hot.

<u>Optional</u>: You can also top with dried Italian seasoning before putting into the oven, or add a sprinkling of cheese of your choice during the last 3 to 4 minutes of cooking time.

Fruit Kabobs

12 grapes
12 strawberries
12 pieces of cantaloupe
12 blueberries

Clean fruit and thread however you like on 6" wooden skewers, using 3 pieces of fruit on each skewer.

Note: This is a great afternoon treat for the children when they come home from school.

Makes 4.

Turkey Nachos

Gluten-free tortilla chips
Shredded cheese
Cooked cut-up turkey

Set oven to 350.

Treat casserole dish with gluten-free non-stick spray. Cover bottom of dish with gluten-free corn tortilla chips.

Pour enough cheese over chips to cover.

Shred or cut up cooked turkey and bake until cheese melts and turkey is hot.

Top with sour cream, tomatoes, black or green olives, and diced onions.

Optional: Substitute regular onions with green onions. This dish can also be fixed in the microwave in place of baked in the oven.

For dairy-free, use Tofutti Sour Supreme.

Deviled Eggs

6 hard-boiled eggs
3 tbs Hellmann's mayonnaise
1 tsp yellow mustard
Sprinkle of salt
Paprika (optional)

Peel the hard-boiled eggs. Cut eggs in half, remove yolks, and place yolks in a separate bowl. Place whites on a serving platter. Add a sprinkle of salt to the yolks. Use the tines of a fork to mash the yolks, then add the mayonnaise and mustard and blend. Spoon the egg yolk mixture into the whites. Sprinkle with paprika if desired.

Serves 6.

Potato Boats

4 medium potatoes
Extra virgin olive oil
Kosher salt
Shredded cheese
Cooked bacon crumbled

Wash and scrub potatoes. Pierce potatoes with a fork in several places. Rub extra virgin olive oil on potatoes and sprinkle with salt. Wrap in aluminum foil and bake at 350 approximately 1 hour or until done.

When potatoes come out of the oven, have your grown-up help you slice them in half and scoop out the insides, leaving approximately 1/4" to 1/2" space. Fill with cheese and top with cooked bacon, and put back into the oven until cheese melts.

Season with salt and pepper, and serve with sour cream, and chives or snipped green onions on top.

Optional: For dairy-free, top with Tofutti Sour Supreme in place of the sour cream.

KIDS IN THE KITCHEN | 11

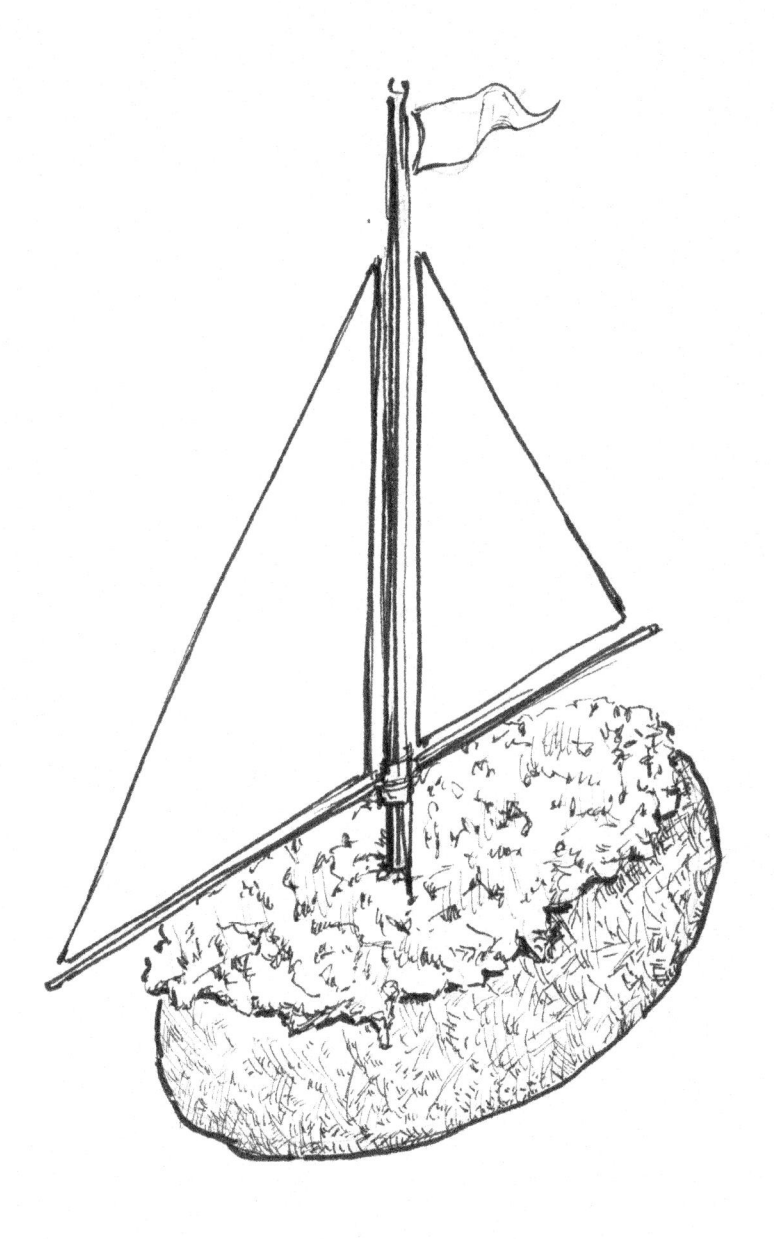

Raw Vegetable Dip

2/3 cup Hellmann's mayonnaise
2/3 cup sour cream
1 tsp dill weed
2 tsp Lawry's seasoned salt
1 tsp onion salt
1/2 tsp gluten-free Worcestershire sauce
4 drops Tabasco (optional)

Mix all ingredients together and store covered in the refrigerator. This keeps for two weeks.

Cut up raw veggies of your choice for dipping. Vegetable choices may include broccoli, celery, carrots, peppers, cauliflower, mushrooms, radishes, etc.

Optional: Use onion powder in place of onion salt.

Sub Tofutti Sour Supreme in place of sour cream for dairy-free.

Chip Dip

8 oz. cream cheese
1/4 tsp garlic powder
1/4 tsp Lawry's seasoned salt
1/4 cup milk
1/2 medium onion diced
Salt and pepper to taste

Beat all ingredients together with a mixer and chill for at least 1 hour.

Use this delicious dip for your gluten-free potato chips, gluten-free pretzels, even veggies. I sometimes even put a dollop onto a baked potato.

Optional: Use 1 to 2 green onions in place of regular onion. For a thicker dip, use less milk.

For dairy-free, replace the cream cheese with Tofutti plain non-dairy cream cheese and add ½ cup Tofutti Sour Supreme and replace milk with dairy-free rice milk.

Beverages

Hot Chocolate

6 tbs unsweetened cocoa
6 tbs sugar
Dash of salt
1/2 cup water
3 cups rice milk
1/2 tsp vanilla

Mix dry ingredients together in a pan. Whisk in water a little at a time to form a paste. Slowly add the milk and cook over medium heat until it starts to boil. Add the vanilla.

Pour into mugs and top with Kraft miniature marshmallows which are gluten-free and dairy-free.

Serves 4.

Chocolate Banana Shakes

1 frozen banana broken into thirds
2 ice cubes
1 cup Blue Diamond Almond Breeze chocolate milk
1 tbs unsweetened cocoa powder

Place all ingredients into a blender and blend until smooth. Serve immediately.

Makes one shake.

Strawberry Shakes

1 cup frozen strawberries
2 ice cubes
1 cup milk

Place all ingredients together in a blender and blend until smooth. Serve immediately.

Optional: For dairy-free, use Blue Diamond vanilla milk.

Note: You may want to add more milk depending on how thick you like your shake.

Strawberry Banana Shakes

1/2 frozen banana cut in chunks
1/2 cup frozen sliced strawberries
1 cup milk

Blend together in a blender 30 to 40 seconds.

<u>Optional:</u> Use 1 cup strawberries for more strawberry taste, which will make this a much thicker shake.

For those going dairy-free, replace the milk with vanilla rice milk or regular rice milk.

Lemonade

7 lemons
1 cup sugar
6 cups water

Roll the lemons on the counter with your hands for a couple of seconds to get the juices flowing. Have your helper cut the lemons in half and squeeze them into a pitcher.

Next add the sugar and the water and stir until sugar is dissolved. Put in the refrigerator and chill.

Serve in ice-filled glasses.

Main Dishes

Grilled Cheese

2 cheese slices
3 tsp butter divided
2 pieces gluten-free bread

Preheat skillet on medium heat. Add one teaspoon of butter.

Spread one teaspoon of butter on each piece of bread.

Top with 2 cheese slices on inside of bread and leave buttered side out. Cook each side approximately 3 to 4 minutes until light brown, checking after three minutes. Time varies depending on how hot your stove temperature is.

Optional: For those going dairy-free, use dairy-free cheese and butter such as a rice cheese or Daiya cheese. Also, butter can be replaced with Earth Balance.

Chili

1 pound ground chuck
1 medium onion chopped
1/2 green pepper chopped
2 cans diced tomatoes (15-16 oz.)
1 tsp sugar
1 can light red kidney beans undrained (15 oz.)
2 to 3 tsp chili powder
1 tsp salt
1 tsp pepper
1/2 tsp ground cumin

Brown the meat, onion, and green pepper on medium heat until done, stirring as needed. Add the rest of the ingredients and bring to a boil. Cover and simmer on medium heat 1 hour or until done, turning down to medium low if needed.

Serves 6.

Optional: You can use any kind of beans you wish in this dish. Undrained pinto or black beans make an excellent choice.

Chili Mac

1 cup uncooked gluten-free macaroni
2 cups boiling salted water
1/2 cup prepared chili

Add uncooked macaroni to 2 cups of boiling salted water and cook for approximately 7-8 minutes. Drain macaroni. Add chili to the macaroni and mix together.

<u>Optional</u> This can be topped with your choice of cheese and put in a preheated 350 degree oven for 5 to 7 minutes or until cheese melts.

Depending on how thick you like your chili mac, you can add a little more pasta or cut down on the amount of chili to make this a thicker dish.

Vegetable Soup

2 tsp olive oil
1/2 cup chopped onion
1 cup chopped carrots
1/2 cup chopped celery
6 cups gluten-free vegetable, beef, or chicken stock
1 can diced tomatoes (15 oz.)
3 medium peeled and diced potatoes
1/2 head cabbage shredded (3-4 cups)
1/2 cup frozen corn
1/2 cup frozen green beans
1/2 cup frozen peas
1 small can tomato sauce (8 oz.)
Salt and pepper to taste

Heat a Dutch oven on medium heat and add the olive oil. Add the onion, carrot, and celery and sauté until soft.

Add the rest of the ingredients and bring to a boil and cover. Turn heat down to low and simmer approximately 2 hours until soup thickens. This makes a nice big kettle of soup.

Optional: You can add any additional veggies of your choosing, such as broccoli, cauliflower, etc. You can also add some stew meat if using beef stock, or chicken if using chicken stock or broth.

My Mom Makes Chicken Noodle Soup

2 bone-in chicken breasts
1 cup sliced carrots
2 stalks celery chopped
1/2 medium onion chopped
12 to 14 cups water
1/2 tsp salt
1/4 tsp pepper
1 1/4 cups Schar Anellini Pasta

Slice the carrots, onions, and celery. Then put everything into the Dutch oven kettle and cover with water. Season with salt and pepper.

Put a lid on the soup pot. Turn the stove onto medium high heat and bring soup to a boil. Reduce heat to medium or medium low and let simmer for a couple of hours.

Once chicken is tender, take the chicken out of the pot and let it cool. When cool enough to handle, remove skin and bones and place chicken back into the pot. Bring to a boil and add the pasta. Cook for approximately 7 to 10 minutes or until done.

Serves 6 to 8.

Optional: In place of the anellini pasta you can use any gluten-free noodle you wish. You may also add 2 tsp of gluten-free chicken base and more salt and pepper if desired.

Pizza

2 gluten-free pizza crusts (I used Udi's)
1/2 cup pizza sauce
Italian seasoning
Pepperoni slices (I used Hormel gluten-free)
1/2 small onion chopped
1/2 cup green and red peppers chopped
1 cup mozzarella cheese

Preheat oven to 375 degrees (if using a brand other than Udi's, refer to instructions on package). Line a cookie sheet with parchment paper and place the crusts on it.

Add your pizza sauce using as much as you desire to the edge of the crust. I used around 1/4 cup for each crust.

Sprinkle with Italian seasoning to taste, followed by pepperoni slices, the onion, and peppers. Top with mozzarella cheese.

Bake for around 8 minutes (or refer to instructions on package for non-Udi's crust).

This was even good warmed up in the oven the next night.

Optional: If going dairy-free, use Daiya vegan mozzarella cheese in place of regular mozzarella cheese.

Baked French Fries

3 medium potatoes peeled and sliced into steak-size fries
Drizzle of vegetable oil
Salt and pepper to taste
Lawry's seasoned salt to taste

Preheat oven to 425 degrees.

Add 1/4 tsp salt to 3 cups of water. Soak sliced potatoes for 10 minutes. You may have to add a little more water if it doesn't cover the potatoes. Drain the water off of the potatoes.

Drizzle a little bit of vegetable oil on a baking sheet that has sides on it.

Spread the potatoes out on the baking sheet. Sprinkle with salt and pepper to taste along with some Lawry's seasoning salt.

Bake for 13 to 15 minutes and turn the potatoes. Bake an additional 13 to 15 minutes or until desired doneness. Drain on paper towels.

Serve plain or with condiment(s) of your choice.

Chicken Loaf

1 pound ground chicken
1 cup soft gluten-free breadcrumbs (2 slices)
1 stalk celery
1 carrot (or 8 small baby cut carrots)
1/4 small onion diced
1 egg
1/8 tsp poultry seasoning
1/4 tsp salt
1/8 tsp pepper
1/2 tsp dried parsley
1/4 cup gluten-free ketchup

Preheat oven to 375 degrees. Line a loaf pan (4 1/2" by 8 1/2)" with aluminum foil and spray with a gluten-free non-stick spray.

Put the two slices of bread in a food processor and pulse into fine crumbs. Take out and set aside. Rough chop the celery, onion, and carrot and put into the food processor and pulse until fine (or dice everything fine by hand).

Mix everything together and put into loaf pan. Bake for 1 to 1 1/2 hours until loaf has a nice brown crust on it. Take out of the oven and let it sit for around 10 minutes. Slice and serve.

For an added treat make a cream sauce to drizzle over the chicken loaf slices.

Cream Sauce

3 tsp butter melted
3 tsp gluten-free flour (I used Namaste perfect flour blend)
2 to 3 cups milk
1 tsp Superior Touch Better Than Bouillon chicken base
Pepper to taste

Whisk together the melted butter and flour on medium heat for approximately a minute or two. Add milk a little at a time, whisking constantly. Add chicken base, still stirring constantly. Season with pepper. Cook until thick and creamy. Serve over chicken loaf slices.

Note: Better Than Bouillon chicken base is gluten-free but does contain dried whey (milk). Substitute a splash of chicken stock if dairy-free and replace butter with Earth Balance and milk with rice milk.

Optional: You can add any amount of shredded cheddar cheese to make an entirely different sauce that can also be served in any macaroni and cheese dish.

Fish Sticks

1 1/4 cups rice flour
1/4 tsp Old Bay Seasoning
1 egg
1/4 cup rice crumbs
1/2 pound fresh cod fish cut into strips (1/2" wide x 1/2" thick, 2-3" long)
1/8 tsp salt
Pepper to taste
3 tbs canola oil

Place flour and Old Bay into a pan. Break the egg into another pan and beat with a fork. Place rice crumbs into a third pan and add the salt and pepper to the crumbs.

Dip the fish strips into the flour mixture and shake off, then into the beaten egg, and finally the crumbs. Heat a skillet on medium heat until hot. Add the fish and cook 3 to 4 minutes until it browns on the bottom and forms a light crust. Turn fish over and cook an additional 3 to 4 minutes. Drain on paper towels.

This recipe can also be baked in a preheated oven at 450 degrees for 15 to 17 minutes, turning halfway through. Do this by laying the fish sticks on a cookie sheet sprayed with a gluten-free vegetable spray and bake as directed.

Optional: Leftovers can be frozen and reheated later in a preheated 450 degree oven for 10 to 15 minutes or until heated through.

Note: I used Orgran gluten-free dairy-free all-purpose rice crumbs.

Chicken Nuggets

1 pound chicken tenders cut into 1" pieces
1/4 cup rice flour
1 egg
1/4 cup rice crumbs
1/4 tsp Lawry's seasoned salt
Pepper to taste
3 tbs canola oil

Place flour in one pan. Break the egg into another pan and beat with a fork. Place the rice crumbs into a third pan. Add the salt and pepper to the flour and mix.

Preheat a 10" skillet on medium heat and add the canola oil, heating until hot.

Dip the chicken pieces into the flour, shaking off the excess, then dip into the beaten egg, and then coat the chicken in the rice crumbs.

Add the coated chicken to the oil, frying 5 to 7 minutes until a brown crust forms. Carefully turn chicken over. Cook an additional 3 to 5 minutes until brown. Drain on paper towels.

Optional: For an Italian-style chicken nugget add 1/4 to 1/2 tsp dried Italian seasoning to crumbs and mix in before frying.

You can also bake instead of fry in a preheated 450 degree oven for 12 minutes, then turn chicken over and bake an additional 7 minutes. Make sure cookie sheet has been sprayed with a gluten-free vegetable spray.

You can also freeze leftovers and reheat in a 450 degree oven for 10 to 15 minutes or until heated through.

Note: I used Orgran gluten-free dairy-free all-purpose rice crumbs.

Pork Chops

2 boneless pork chops
Gluten-free flour
1 egg
1 1/2 cups gluten-free Kellogg's Rice Krispies
3 to 4 tbs canola oil
Salt and pepper

Tenderize your chops into cutlets by placing plastic wrap over the chop, which has been placed on a chopping block board. Pound until 1/4" thin. Make sure to wash your hands when done.

Prepare the crumb coating by placing the gluten-free Rice Krispies in a quart bag and rolling a rolling pin over them until they are crushed, then pour onto a plate. Break the egg into a dish big enough to hold the pork chops, and beat the egg. Pour some gluten-free flour onto another plate.

Preheat a 10" skillet on medium heat and put the oil in. Coat the chops in the flour and shake off excess, then dip into the beaten egg, followed by the crumb mixture. Place them in the preheated skillet. Season with salt and pepper. Cook for approximately 7 minutes until golden brown and have helper turn them over. Continue to cook for an additional 6 to 7 minutes until cooked through. Transfer them to a serving plate.

Serves 3 to 4.

<u>Optional</u>: Add a sprinkling of Lawry's Seasoned Salt in place of regular salt for additional flavor.

Spaghetti with Marinara Sauce

2 tbs extra virgin olive oil
1/4 small onion diced
2 tsp garlic minced
2 cans gluten-free diced or crushed tomatoes (28 oz.)
2 tsp dried basil
1 tsp dried oregano
2 tsp dried parsley

1 box gluten-free spaghetti
Parmesan cheese

In a large skillet add oil, onion, and garlic on medium heat. Cook until soft. Add the rest of the ingredients (except spaghetti and parmesan) and cook until sauce starts to bubble, then reduce heat to low and simmer for 20 to 25 minutes.

Cook pasta according to package directions and drain. Pour the marinara sauce over the drained spaghetti. Sprinkle parmesan cheese over the spaghetti.

Optional: You may use fresh basil and parsley in place of dried. Just use a little extra if using the fresh herbs.

If you are going dairy-free, omit the parmesan cheese, or use dairy-free parmesan cheese such as Vegan Grated Topping made by Galaxy Nutritional Foods.

Meatballs

1/2 pound ground chuck
2 tsp fresh rosemary chopped
3 tsp fresh basil chopped
3 tsp fresh parsley chopped
1/4 medium onion diced
1/2 cup gluten-free oats
Salt and pepper to taste

Preheat oven to 350 degrees.

Mix everything together in one bowl and form into 1" meatballs. Place the meatballs onto an ungreased baking sheet and place into the preheated oven, baking for 25 to 30 minutes.

The number of meatballs this makes depends on the size you make them. This gives me 8 to 10 meatballs.

Optional: You may substitute dried herbs for fresh ones, but cut down by 1 teaspoon each.

You may also use rice cracker crumbs in place of the gluten-free oats.

Serve alone, or add to a marinara sauce for meatball subs or spaghetti.

Macaroni and Cheese

1 1/2 cups gluten-free pasta
4 cups water
1 tsp salt
1 recipe cheese sauce
Gluten-free bread crumbs

Preheat oven to 350 degrees.

Measure the water into a 6 quart pan. Place the pan on stove at medium high heat and bring to a boil. Add the salt. Cook pasta according to package directions and drain. Add the cheese sauce and mix together over medium low heat until coated.

Spray a casserole dish with cooking spray and pour macaroni and cheese into the casserole dish. Top with a sprinkling of gluten-free bread crumbs. Place in preheated oven and bake 25 to 30 minutes.

Optional: Add a few chopped green onions along with 1 cup of cooked chopped chicken before baking for additional flavor.

Cheese Sauce

4 tbs olive oil
4 tbs sweet rice flour
2 1/2 cups milk
4 tbs nutritional yeast
1 tsp salt
1/8 tsp garlic powder
1/4 tsp dried minced onion
1 tsp gluten-free Dijon mustard
1 tbs rice vinegar
1/4 tsp nutmeg
1/2 tsp paprika
1/2 tbs sesame oil
2 oz. cheddar cheese cubed

Heat olive oil over medium heat until hot and whisk in the flour. Cook and stir for around 30 seconds to 1 minute until raw flour is cooked out. Slowly whisk in the milk and bring to a boil, then reduce heat to low. Whisk in the rest of the ingredients and cook until thick and bubbly.

Makes approximately 3 cups.

Optional: If going dairy-free, use rice milk in place of regular milk and use 1 oz Vegan Gourmet Cheese in place of 2 oz. of cheddar cheese.

Sloppy Joes

2 1/2 pounds ground beef or ground chuck
1/2 cup chopped green pepper
1 small onion diced
2 1/2 cups gluten-free tomato sauce
1 1/4 cups gluten-free ketchup
2 1/2 tbs firmly packed light brown sugar
2 1/2 tbs yellow mustard (may use Dijon for more of a kick)
1/2 tsp salt
1/4 tsp pepper
2 1/2 tbs gluten-free Worcestershire sauce
2 tbs apple cider or white vinegar

Brown the ground beef, green pepper, and onion together in a Dutch oven over medium to medium high heat and drain.

Add the rest of the ingredients and cook on medium to medium high heat until hot. Reduce heat to low and simmer 30 to 45 minutes, stirring occasionally.

Serve on gluten-free buns or bread.

Optional: For a thicker Sloppy Joe, add some rice cracker crumbs or 1 tsp of tomato paste to mixture while simmering.

Salmon Patties

1 can salmon drained (14.75 oz.)
25 to 35 small rice crackers crushed and rolled out with a rolling pin
1 egg
2 tbs extra virgin olive oil or shortening

Remove bones from salmon. Mix salmon, crackers, and egg together and shape into 4 patties. Fry in oil or shortening on medium heat until crust forms. Turn over and put a lid on to finish steaming until crust forms on other side.

Serves 4.

These are great served with fried potatoes and a side of peas.

Optional: You may use boxed gluten-free cracker crumbs in place of rolling out your own crackers. Use around 1/4 cup to get started to see if patties stick together; you can always add more, but you can't take it away.

Tacos

6 gluten-free taco shells
1 pound ground chuck or ground turkey
1/2 medium onion diced
2 tbs gluten-free taco seasoning
3 to 4 tbs water
Shredded lettuce
Diced tomatoes
Cheddar cheese

Brown ground chuck or turkey and onion in a skillet over medium low heat until cooked through. Add the taco seasoning and water and cook 3 to 4 minutes. Spread taco mixture inside taco shells followed by lettuce, tomatoes, and cheddar cheese.

Optional: You may use the toppings of your choice or add to the ones I have given you.

You can also add 3 tbs of gluten-free taco seasoning from this book and stir in 2/3 cup of the cooked beef or turkey and simmer until most of the water has evaporated.

Taco Seasoning

1 tbs plus 1 tsp chili powder
2 tsp onion powder
1/4 tsp ground cumin
1 tsp garlic powder
1 tsp dried oregano
1 tsp sugar
1/2 tsp salt

Mix together and store in a cool, dry place. When ready to use, sprinkle over cooked drained hamburger and stir in 2/3 cup of water and simmer until most of the liquid has evaporated.

Beanie Weenies

1 can vegetarian pork and beans undrained (15 to 16 oz.)
2 to 3 heaping tsp light brown sugar
1 to 2 tsp diced onion
2 tbs gluten-free ketchup
2 gluten-free hotdogs sliced into 1" pieces (I prefer Hebrew National)

Mix all ingredients together and cook until hot dogs and beans are cooked through.

Optional: As an added treat, top with cooked crumbled bacon.

Serve with a side of Oven Baked Fries.

Quesadillas

2 tbs extra virgin olive oil
1/2 medium onion
1/2 medium pepper
1 small chicken breast cooked and shredded
Shredded cheese
Gluten-free vegetable spray

Preheat a 10" skillet and add the oil, onion, and green pepper. Cook until soft. Add the shredded chicken and cook until heated through. Take out the chicken mixture and set aside. Wipe out the skillet with a paper towel and spray with gluten-free vegetable spray. Turn heat to medium. Lay down a corn tortilla and put a couple heaping teaspoons of chicken veggie mixture. Top with a sprinkling of shredded cheese of your choice. Add another tortilla on top and cook for 2 to 3 minutes on each side or until golden brown, then turn over, doing the same to the other side. Press down with a spatula and watch closely until cheese is melted. Remove from heat. Do the same with the rest of your corn tortillas and chicken veggie mixture. Cut across one way and then the opposite way to make 4 triangles for each tortilla.

Optional: For dairy-free I like to use Daiya shredded cheese.

Baked Chicken Patties

1 lb. ground chicken
1 stalk celery minced
1/4 medium onion minced
1 tsp dried parsley minced
1/4 tsp salt
4 tbs gluten-free flour (I used Namaste Perfect Flour Blend)
1/4 cup Egg Beaters
1 cup Corn Chex crumbs

Preheat oven to 375 degrees. Spray a 9x13 cake pan with gluten-free vegetable spray.

Mix chicken, celery, onion, parsley, and salt together. Shape into 6 patties and set aside. Place flour into one bowl, the Egg Beaters in a second bowl, and the Corn Chex crumbs in a third bowl. Dredge the patties in the flour, then the egg mixture, and finally into the crumbs. Place into prepared pan. Bake on center rack for 35 to 40 minutes, turning halfway through.

These can be pan fried in a small amount of olive oil if you wish.

Optional: Replace the Egg Beaters with 1 egg. You can also season with salt and pepper in place of just salt.

Breakfast

French Toast

4 eggs
4 tbs milk
4 pieces gluten-free bread
2 tbs butter or margarine
Warm maple syrup

Melt butter in a skillet over medium low heat. Whisk eggs with milk. Dip bread into custard mixture, coating each side. Fry in melted butter until a crust forms on one side, then flip toast over and do the same on the other side. Serve with warm maple syrup.

Serves 2

Optional: Sprinkle cinnamon into egg custard before dipping bread. You also may serve with butter on top of French toast before adding syrup and sprinkle with powdered sugar for an additional treat.

For dairy-free use rice milk and vegan butter or margarine of your choice.

Pancakes

1/2 cup gluten-free flour (I used Namaste)
1/2 cup cream of rice
1 tbs baking powder
1 egg
1 cup milk
2 tbs melted butter

Mix the flour, cream of rice, and baking powder together and set aside.

Mix the egg, milk and melted butter until blended.

Add the wet ingredients to the dry ingredients, mixing just until blended. Let stand 4 to 5 minutes. The longer this sits the thicker it will get.

Lightly grease skillet or griddle on medium heat. Drop by big heaping tablespoons into hot skillet. Cook 2 to 3 minutes or until bubbles are over the top of the pancake, then flip over and cook an additional 2 to 3 minutes.

Makes approximately 10 to 15 pancakes depending on how big you make them.

Drizzle with warm maple syrup.

Note: You may want to thin with a little extra milk if batter gets too thick.

Optional: If going dairy-free, replace butter with Earth Balance and the milk with rice milk.

Sausage Gravy

Spray a skillet with cooking spray

Cook the following together on medium to medium high heat. (If sausage starts to stick to the skillet, you may need to add 1 to 2 tsp shortening or bacon grease.)

1 lb. sausage
1 tsp sage
1/2 tsp poultry seasoning
1/4 tsp herbs de provence
1 to 1 1/4 tsp salt
1/4 tsp pepper
Pinch of savory
2 tbs gluten-free flour
1 tsp butter
3 cups milk (approximate)

Cook sausage, sage, poultry seasoning, herbs de provence, salt, pepper, and savory until sausage is fully cooked and crumbled. Add the flour (I use Bob's Red Mill Gluten Free Flour). Stir to make a roux. Cook about 1 minute until all flour is absorbed. Add the butter.

Add milk a little at a time, stirring constantly, until you get the desired consistency. Keep stirring until hot and bubbly. Season with additional salt and pepper to taste.

Serves 3 to 4.

My husband loves this over fried potatoes or gluten-free toast points.

Optional: If going dairy-free, replace the butter with Earth Balance and the milk with rice milk.

SCRAMBLED EGGS

8 eggs
1/4 cup milk
2 tbs butter
Salt and pepper to taste

Melt butter in a skillet. Whisk eggs and milk together and pour into the skillet. Add salt and pepper to taste. Cook on low to medium low heat, stirring frequently, until cooked through, or until they reach the consistency you like.

Serves 3 to 4.

Optional: Add a small amount of diced onion or green pepper for added flavor while cooking. Also cooked diced ham or bacon is a treat to stir in.

Replace the butter with Earth Balance and the milk with rice milk if going dairy-free.

Hole in One

1 piece gluten-free bread
1 egg
Very small pinch of salt
Butter

Preheat a non-stick skillet on medium low heat. Cut out the middle of the bread with a round cookie cutter of your choice. Butter the bread, plus the middle piece you took out, on both sides. Lay the bread in the skillet and add a small amount of butter in the hole. Once it melts, crack the egg open and put it inside the bread. Lay the extra bread you cut out of the middle in the pan also. Cook 2 to 3 minutes on one side and carefully turn it over. Cook an additional 2 minutes on the other side. Watch closely so the bread doesn't burn. Your cook time will depend on how hot your pan gets on the burner.

Once done, carefully remove to a plate and use the round piece of bread as your dipper, then use the outsides of the bread also to dip into the yolk.

<u>Optional:</u> Use Earth Balance if going dairy-free.

Banana Muffins

Wet ingredients
3 medium bananas mashed
1/2 cup cinnamon applesauce
1/2 cup brown sugar packed
2 tsp vanilla
2 eggs
1/3 cup soymilk
1/3 cup vegetable oil

Dry ingredients
1/4 cup cornstarch
1 cup sorghum flour
1/2 cup rice flour
1/4 cup almond meal
1/2 tsp salt
2 tsp baking powder
1 tsp baking soda
1 tsp xanthan gum
1 tsp cinnamon

Preheat oven to 350 degrees. Line muffin pan with paper liners.

Mix the wet ingredients together. Whisk the dry ingredients together and add to the wet ingredients. Add 1/4 cupful to each muffin cup and bake for 20 to 25 minutes or until a wooden toothpick comes out clean when inserted into the center of the muffin. Once the muffins cool, dust with powdered sugar.

Makes 12 to 18 muffins depending on the size muffin pan you are using.

Optional: Add 3 or 4 pecan pieces pushed down in each muffin.

Desserts

Chocolate Chip Cookies

1 cup butter flavor Crisco shortening
3/4 cup granulated sugar
3/4 cup packed brown sugar
1 tsp vanilla
2 eggs
2 1/4 cup gluten-free flour mix
1 tsp baking soda
1 tsp salt
1 tsp xanthan gum
12 oz. gluten-free chocolate chips

Preheat oven to 375 degrees.

Beat shortening, sugars, and vanilla together until creamy. Add eggs one at a time, beating well after each addition. Mix the baking mix, soda, salt, and xanthan gum. Gradually beat flour mixture into creamed mixture. Stir in chocolate chips. Dough will be stiff. Drop by teaspoonfuls onto ungreased baking sheets. Bake 8 to 9 minutes until lightly brown. Cool on baking sheets 1 minute and remove to wax paper to finish cooling. Store in an airtight container.

Makes approximately 6 dozen cookies.

Note: You can use dairy-free gluten-free chocolate chips made by Tropical Source. Look for UPC 2958201281 (10 oz package). I found them at Healthy Alternative in Dayton, Ohio: (937) 890-8000 or www.healthyalternativemarkets.com

Also, chocolate chips can be ordered from Chocolate Decadence (www.chocolatedecadence.com).

Chocolate Pudding

3 tbs cornstarch
1/3 cup sugar
1/2 tsp salt
3 tbs cocoa
2 cups chocolate soy milk divided
1 tsp vanilla

Whisk dry ingredients together and add 1/2 cup of the milk, whisking until smooth. Add the rest of the soy milk on medium to medium high heat until hot but not boiling. Whisk in the cocoa mixture, stirring constantly until mixture thickens and just starts to come to a boil. Remove from heat and stir in the vanilla. Put in pudding dishes, let cool, and refrigerate.

Serves 4.

May be served warm or cold.

<u>Optional:</u> You can also make this with rice milk in place of chocolate soy milk, but it won't taste as chocolaty. For those going with regular dairy, just substitute the soy/rice milk for regular milk.

Rice Chex Cereal Bars

4 tbs Earth Balance vegan butter
10 oz. Kraft Jet Puffed Marshmallows
6 cups Rice Chex cereal slightly crushed
1 tsp vanilla (optional)

Melt butter in a large Dutch kettle pan on medium heat. Add marshmallows, stirring occasionally until marshmallows are melted. Add vanilla if you are using it. Remove from heat and add Rice Chex cereal, stirring until coated. Press into a buttered 13x9x2 pan. Cut into squares when cool.

Makes 24 squares (2" each).

Note:
Rice Chex cereal is a gluten-free, dairy-free product from General Mills. I talked to Marsha at 800-328-1144 on October 2nd, 2009 and she confirmed this.

Kraft Jet Puffed Marshmallows are a gluten-free, dairy-free product. I talked to Cecelia from Kraft at 800-431-1001 on October 2nd, 2009 and she confirmed this.

Rice Krispie Treats

3 1/2 tbs butter
6 cups mini marshmallows
7 cups gluten-free Kellogg's Rice Krispies
1 tsp vanilla

Butter the bottom and sides of a 9x13 cake pan. Melt butter over medium low heat until melted through. Add marshmallows, stirring until melted. Take the pan off the heat and stir in the vanilla. Add the Rice Krispies and stir until coated.

Pour into prepared cake pan and press into pan. Let cool and cut into squares.

Makes 24 squares depending on how big you cut them.

Optional: If going dairy-free, exchange the butter for a vegan butter such as Earth Balance.

Chocolate Brownies

8 tbs butter
3/4 cup unsweetened dark cocoa
2 eggs
1 cup packed brown sugar
1/2 cup almond meal
1/4 cup rice flour
1/2 tsp salt
1/4 tsp baking powder
1/4 cup gluten-free, dairy-free semi chocolate chips

Preheat oven to 350 degrees. Line an 8x8 pan with aluminum foil and lightly oil bottom of foil.

Melt butter (I use a microwave at 50% power for 55 seconds then stir, repeat process). Stir the cocoa into the melted butter until blended. Set aside. Beat the eggs on medium high until foamy. Add the brown sugar and beat again until smooth. Add the chocolate mixture a little at a time into the egg mixture on medium speed until smooth and glossy.

Whisk the dry ingredients together and add to the chocolate mixture. Mix on medium speed until all blended. Pour into prepared pan. Sprinkle chocolate chips over the top of the brownie mixture and push down slightly. Shake pan gently to smooth everything to the edges. Bake 30 to 35 minutes. Check at 30 minutes with a toothpick inserted in the middle of brownie mixture. This is best if under-baked slightly. Let cool and cut into squares. This produces a cake-like brownie the first day, then a more fudge-type brownie after sitting overnight.

Makes 9 to 12 squares depending on how big you cut them.

Optional: Sprinkle some pecans over the top with the chocolate chips and push down into mixture.

For dairy-free, use vegan butter such as Earth Balance in place of regular butter.

Gluten-Free Flour Mix

6 cups rice flour
2 cups potato starch
1 cup tapioca flour

Sift all ingredients together and store in an airtight container.

Where to Find Gluten-Free and Dairy-Free Supplies

A Bushel & A Peck Bulk Foods,
9515 Haber Road, Clayton, OH 45315
Phone: (937) 836-4997
Wheat-free, gluten-free flours, spices, natural foods, nutritional products.

Arrowhead Mills, Inc.,
P.O. Box 2059,
Herford, TX 79045
Phone: (800) 364-0730
Wheat-free, gluten-free flours, oils, mixes, etc.

Bob's Red Mill Natural Foods,
5209 S.E. International Way,
Milwaukie, OR 97222
Phone: (503) 654-3215
www.bobsredmill.com
Wheat-free, gluten-free flours, baking mixes, and other products.

Dorothy Lane Market,
2710 Far Hills Ave,
Centerville, OH 45419
Phone: (937) 299-3561
(866) 278-3561
Fax: (937) 299-3568
www.dorothylane.com
Wheat-free, gluten-free products, etc.

Earth Balance, GFA Brands, Inc.,
P.O. Box 397,
Cresskill, NJ 07626
Phone: (201) 568-9300
www.earthbalance.net
Wheat-free, gluten-free, dairy-free products, margarines, butters, and spreads.

Ener-G foods, Inc.,
P.O. Box 84487,
Seattle, WA 98124
Phone: (800) 331-5222
Fax: (206) 764-3398
Wheat-free, gluten-free flours, egg-replacer, dry mixes, cereals, etc.

Food For Life Baking Company,
P.O. Box 1434,
Corona, CA 92878
Phone: 800-797-5090
Fax: (909) 279-1784
www.foodforlife.com
Gluten-free breads, pasta, etc. Some of these products can be found in natural food stores.

Galaxy Nutritional Foods
Phone: (407) 855-5500
www.galaxyfoods.com
Healthy Alternative Natural Food Markets,
8258 North Main Street,
Dayton, OH 45415
Phone: (937) 890-8000
www.healthyalternativemarkets.com
Wheat-free, gluten-free, dairy-free products, mixes, etc.

Kroger,
855 Union Blvd,
Englewood, OH 45322
Phone: (937) 832-4060
Wheat-free, gluten-free flours, mixes, cereals, other products.

Kroger,
780 Northwoods Blvd,
Vandalia, OH 45377
Phone: (937) 264-2400
Wheat-free, gluten-free flours, mixes, cereals, other products.

Meijer Inc,
9200 N. Main Street,
Englewood, OH 45322
Phone: (937) 832-5101
Wheat-free, gluten-free products, cereals, other products.

Madhava Honey,
P.O. Box 756,
Lyons, Colorado 80540
Phone: (303) 823-5166
http://www.madhavasweeteners.com
Wheat-free, gluten-free, pure organic agave nectar sugar alternative.

Nutraceutical Corporation,
1400 Kearns Blvd.,
Second Floor,
Park City, UT 84060
Phone: (800) 669-8877
www.nutraceutical.com
Wheat-free, gluten-free, dairy-free products, nutritional yeast flakes

Trader Joe's,
328 E Stroop Road,
Dayton, OH 45429-2828
Phone: (937) 294-5411
www.traderjoes.com
Wheat-free, gluten-free, dairy-free products, cereals, breads, etc.

West Milton IGA,
1177 South Miami Street,
West Milton, OH 45383
Phone: (937) 698-4206
Wheat-free, gluten-free products, cereals, other products.

Walmart,
465 York Commons Blvd,
Dayton, OH 45414
Phone: (937) 454-6240
Wheat-free, gluten-free products, cereals, etc.

Walmart,
7725 Hoke Road,
Englewood, OH 45315
Phone: (937) 836-9405
Wheat-free, gluten-free products, cereals, etc.

Walmart,
1801 West Main Street,
Troy, OH 45373
Phone: (937) 339-7211
Wheat-free, gluten-free products, cereals, etc.

This list is for the reader's convenience. I regret I cannot be responsible for changes in names, addresses, or phone numbers, or for companies removing any products from this line.

Measurements

1 tablespoon = 3 teaspoons

1 fluid ounce = 2 tablespoons

1 jigger = 3 tablespoons

1/4 cup = 4 tablespoons

1/3 cup = 5 1/3 tablespoons

1/2 cup = 8 tablespoons

2/3 cup = 10 2/3 tablespoons

3/4 cup = 12 tablespoons

1 cup = 1/2 pint or 16 tablespoons or 8 fluid ounces

1 pint = 2 cups

1 quart = 4 cups or 2 pints

1/2 gallon = 2 quarts

1 gallon = 4 quarts

8 quarts = 1 peck

4 pecks = 1 bushel

2 tablespoons butter = 1 ounce

1/2 stick butter = 4 tablespoons or 1/4 cup

1 stick butter = 8 tablespoons or 1/2 cup

1 pound butter = 4 sticks or 2 cups

1 pound = 16 ounces

Oven Chart

Very Slow Oven = 250 to 275 degrees

Slow Oven = 300 to 325 degrees

Moderate Oven = 350 to 375 degrees

Hot Oven = 400 to 425 degrees

Very Hot Oven = 450 to 475 degrees

Extremely Hot Oven = 500 to 525 degrees

THERMOMETER READINGS
TEMPERATURE FOR MEATS

BEEF
Rare 140 degrees
Medium 160 degrees
Well-done 170 degrees

POULTRY
Open pan 195 degrees
In foil 190 degrees

FRESH PORK 185 degrees

LAMB 170 to 180 degrees

VEAL 170 degrees

About the Author

Janet Wheelock Balsbaugh lives in the rural community of West Milton, Ohio where she was raised on a farm. Janet lives with her husband Jim, and her cat Miss Daisey. She has two grown daughters and three grandsons. Janet's love of cooking has inspired her to write her cookbooks. She has one cookbook out called Home-Style Gluten Free And Dairy Free Cookbook and now a children's gluten free cookbook called Kid's In The Kitchen, Cooking Gluten Free.